Civic Skills and Values

Sharing

By Dalton Rains

www.littlebluehousebooks.com

Copyright © 2024 by Little Blue House, Mendota Heights, MN 55120. All rights reserved. No part of this book may be reproduced or utilized in any form or by any means without written permission from the publisher.

Little Blue House is distributed by North Star Editions:
sales@northstareditions.com | 888-417-0195

Produced for Little Blue House by Red Line Editorial.

Photographs ©: Shutterstock Images, cover, 4, 7, 11, 12, 15, 16, 18–19, 21, 22–23, 24 (top left), 24 (top right), 24 (bottom right); iStockphoto, 9, 24 (bottom left)

Library of Congress Control Number: 2022919838

ISBN
978-1-64619-822-1 (hardcover)
978-1-64619-851-1 (paperback)
978-1-64619-907-5 (ebook pdf)
978-1-64619-880-1 (hosted ebook)

Printed in the United States of America
Mankato, MN
082023

About the Author

Dalton Rains writes and edits nonfiction children's books. He lives in Minnesota.

Table of Contents

Sharing Is Caring **5**

Struggles **13**

Many Ways **17**

Glossary **24**

Index **24**

Sharing Is Caring

Sharing is about giving.

It can help other people.

You can share toys with your sister.
Sharing shows her that you care.

You can share your doll with a friend.
It can help you become better friends.

You can also share

in class.

You could share

your crayons.

Then others can draw.

Struggles

Sometimes it is hard to share. You might want to keep something for yourself.

But sharing can be fun.
You can let other people
use your ball.
Then you can play a
game with them.

Many Ways

There are many ways
to share.

You can share a phone.

You can both listen to music.

You can share video games. Taking turns lets everyone play.

You might have things
you do not need.
You can share them
with others.

Sharing is important.
It can help others.
Sharing shows people
that you care.

Glossary

class

phone

friend

video games

Index

B
ball, 14

D
doll, 8

M
music, 17

S
sister, 6